UTAH
REFLECTIONS

Photography by Tom Till
With Selected Prose & Poetry

Utah Littlebooks

Westcliffe Publishers, Inc., Englewood, Colorado

First frontispiece: Castle Rock, Grand County
Second frontispiece: Sunrise at Rainbow Park, Dinosaur National Monument
Third frontispiece: Salt Wash Canyon, Colorado River
Opposite: Salt formations near Stansbury Island, Great Salt Lake

International Standard Book Number: 1-56579-141-X
Library of Congress Catalog Number: 95-62426
Copyright Tom Till, 1996. All rights reserved.
Published by Westcliffe Publishers, Inc.
2650 South Zuni Street, Englewood, Colorado 80110
Publisher, John Fielder; Editor, Suzanne Venino; Designer, Amy Duenkel
Printed in Hong Kong by Palace Press

PREFACE

The waters of Utah, though they may be few and far between in one of the country's driest states, reflect some of the most compelling scenery in the world. Utahns and visitors alike are drawn to the few water courses of the state, whether they be in the often icy waters of lakes in the High Uinta Wilderness, or the tepid waters of a summer pothole in Canyonlands National Park. The story of these reflections, vibrant and saturated by the clean, dry desert air, is really the story of water, exalted and appreciated in this dessicated world wherever it occurs.

One of the most famous lakes in the Uinta Mountains is Mirror Lake, so named for its faithful reflection of the surrounding peaks. Sometimes the faithfulness of the reflection in still water is so great that it is difficult to tell where the reflection ends and reality begins.

My ancestors from the British Isles were greatly moved by the mirrorlike reflections they often saw in the lochs of coastal mountains. In their legends and folklore, the reflections were doors to other fantastic worlds, populated by mythical creature and ferocious beasts. We don't, of course, believe these stories in the 20th century, but most people can understand the attraction and the otherworldly appeal when they rise early and stand at the shore of a high mountain lake to view a perfect reflection through the morning mists.

Some of the greatest reflection photographs of Utah were taken by the peerless landscape photographer Eliot Porter in Glen Canyon, now lost under the waters of Lake Powell. Phillip Hyde, another great landscape photographer, has said that the Colorado Plateau reached its ultimate in two places, each with its own separate and distinct personality. One was the Grand Canyon, the other Glen Canyon. In a few nameless canyons, where small streams pour over silver and blue limestone and nurture hanging gardens of ferns and monkeyflowers, the now-vanished echo of

Leaves in the Virgin River, Zion National Park

Glen Canyon survives. As one walks through one of these canyons on a hot summer evening, reflections are everywhere, turning the plunge pools and rivulets to a dense sparkling gold.

Some of these quiet reflecting pools are more dangerous than their tranquil beauty indicates. Last summer, after photographing a small, shallow, spring-fed pool tucked in a limestone canyon, I slipped into the water to gain relief from the 115-degree temperature. I was immediately in trouble. Though it was mid-June, the water in the deep canyon was numbingly cold. Within seconds I lost feeling in my legs, and I struggled in vain to move them and climb out of the pool.

What normally would have been a simple task of climbing quickly out of the frigid waters was made impossible by the hidden, moss-covered, and concave sides of the reflecting pool. Though I struggled and worked to pull myself out of the debilitating trough, I would have died in the innocently tranquil waters if my hiking companion had not quickly rescued me.

The dangers notwithstanding, reflections will continue to be subjects that excite and inspire me, and they afford me opportunities to make unusual images of Utah subjects, like Delicate Arch, that have been photographed by hundreds of professional photographers and perhaps millions of amateurs. Finding a new way to interpret an icon of the American landscape such as that famous sandstone span is a piece of luck that may come along only a few times in a photographer's lifetime.

I also find it a fascinating coincidence that the water that created the world's most magnificently eroded landscape provides me and the viewer with a new way to see and experience this singular landscape. Each arch and canyon, each river and reflecting plunge pool all bear out the famous quote from naturalist Loren Eisley, "If there is magic on this planet, it is contained in water."

— Tom Till
Moab, Utah

Zion Narrows reflection, Zion National Park

"Nature is an endless combination and repetition of a very few laws. She hums the old well-known air through innumerable variations."

— Ralph Waldo Emerson, *Essays*

Moab Sloughs, Scott Matheson Nature Conservancy Preserve

"How often we forget all time, when lone
Admiring Nature's universal throne
Her woods, her wilds, her waters intense
Reply of hers to our intelligence."

— Lord Byron, *The Island*

Manti-La Sal National Forest, Wasatch Range

"Nature has presented us with a large faculty of entertaining ourselves alone…to teach us that we owe ourselves in part to society, but chiefly and mostly to ourselves."

— Montaigne, *On Giving the Lie*

Hovenweep Castle, Hovenweep National Monument

"There is a road from the eye to the heart
that does not go through the intellect."

— G. K. Chesterton, *The Defendant*

Limestone "streets," Glen Canyon National Recreation Area

"A rock pile ceases to be a rock pile the moment a
single man contemplates it, bearing within him
the image of a cathedral."

— Antoine de Saint-Exupery, *Flight of Arras*

Taylor Creek, Zion National Park

Overleaf: Sunset over Great Salt Lake, Great Salt Lake State Park

"Solitude...is essential to any depth of meditation or of character; and solitude in the presence of natural beauty and grandeur, is the cradle of thoughts and aspirations..."

— John Stuart Mill, *Principles of Political Economy*

Delicate Arch, Arches National Park

"What would the world be, one bereft
Of wet and of wildness? Let them be left,
O let them be left, wildness and wet;
Long live the weeds and the wilderness yet."

— Gerard Manley Hopkins, *Inversnaid*

Stream bank grasses, Gold Bar Canyon

"The day, water, sun, moon, night — I do not have
to purchase these things with money."

— Titus Maccius Plautus, *The Comedy of Asses*

Sunset on Lake Powell,
Glen Canyon National Recreation Area

"Now I see the secret of the making of the best persons. It is to grow in the open air, and to eat and sleep with the earth."

— Walt Whitman, *Leaves of Grass*

Rabbitbrush, Ashley National Forest

"The chess-board is the world, the pieces are the phenomena of the universe, the rules of the game are what we call the laws of Nature."

— T. H. Huxley, *A Liberal Education*

Split Mountain Canyon, on the Green River,
Dinosaur National Monument

"To the attentive eye, each moment of the year has its own beauty...it beholds, every hour, a picture which was never seen before, and which shall never be seen again."

— Ralph Waldo Emerson, *Beauty*

Morning Glory Pool, Negro Bill Canyon Wilderness Study Area

"Everybody needs beauty as well as bread,
places to play in and pray in where Nature
may heal and cheer and give strength to the
body and soul alike."

— John Muir, *Travels in Alaska*

The Colorado River, Westwater Canyon Wilderness Study Area

Overleaf: Late snow and aspen trees, Ashley National Forest

"Every situation — nay, every moment — is of
infinite worth, for it is the representative
of a whole eternity."

— Goethe, in Eckermann's *Conversations*

Lake Powell, Glen Canyon National Recreation Area

"Everything that happens happens as it should,
and if you observe carefully,
you will find this to be so."

— Marcus Aurelius, *Meditations*

Ice formations on the Colorado River, Grand County

"To see clearly is poetry, prophecy,
and religion — all in one."

— John Ruskin, *Modern Painters*

Cecret Lake, Wasatch National Forest

"And many standing round a waterfall
See one rainbow each, yet not the same to all,
But each a hand's breadth further than the next
The sun on falling waters writes the text..."

— Gerard Manley Hopkins, *At a Welsh Waterfall*

Bridalveil Falls, Provo Canyon,
Uinta National Forest

"The whole secret of the study of nature lies in learning how to use one's eyes..."

— George Sand, *Nouvelles Lettres d'un Voyageur*

Courthouse Towers, Arches National Park

"The visible marks of extraordinary…
power appears so plainly in all the works of
creation that a rational creature who will but
seriously reflect on them cannot miss the
discovery of a deity."

— John Locke,
An Essay Concerning Human Understanding

Red Castle Peak, High Uintas Wilderness

"We do not receive wisdom,
we have to discover it for ourselves
by a voyage that no one can take for us…"

— Marcel Proust, *Remembrance of Things Past*

Falls on Mill Creek, La Sal Mountains

Overleaf: Sunset along the Highline Trail, High Uintas Wilderness

"To him who in the love of Nature holds
Communion with her visible forms, she speaks
A various language."

— William Cullen Bryant, *Thanatopsis*

Courthouse Wash, Arches National Park

"It is the marriage of the soul with Nature that makes the intellect fruitful, and gives birth to the imagination."

— Henry David Thoreau, *Journal*

San Juan River through Slickhorn Canyon,
Glen Canyon National Recreation Area

"And forget not that the earth delights to feel your bare feet and the winds long to play with your hair."

— Kahlil Gibran, *The Prophet*

Christmas Meadows, High Unitas Wilderness

"We need the tonic of wildness...
We can never have enough of nature
We must be refreshed by the sight of inexhaustible vigor,
vast and titanic features..."

— Henry David Thoreau, *Walden*

Evening light on the Colorado River, upriver of Monument Canyon,
Canyonlands National Park

Stevens Arch reflected in the Escalante River,
Glen Canyon National Recreation Area